GW01458874

BOOK ANALYSIS

By Candice Kent

The Good Soldier
BY FORD MADOX FORD

Bright
≡Summaries.com

FORD MADOX FORD

ENGLISH NOVELIST, POET AND EDITOR

- **Born in Surrey in 1873.**
- **Died in Deauville in 1939.**
- **Notable works:**
  - *The Inheritors* (1901), novel (cowritten with Joseph Conrad)
  - *The Fifth Queen* (1906-1908), historical novel trilogy
  - *Parade's End* (1924-1928), novel tetralogy

Ford Madox Ford, formerly Ford Madox Heuffer, had parents with both artistic and musical connections. As a consequence, he grew up surrounded by the intellectual and cultural elite of his time. Ford eloped with Elsie Martindale in 1894, but suffered a breakdown from stress caused by the disintegration of his relationship with his wife, aggravated by financial difficulties, in 1904. Following a relationship with the writer Violet Hunt, Ford departed for France, where he lived with the painter Stella Bowen. After World War I he changed his last name from the German Heuffer to Ford.

Throughout his life Ford was a prolific writer of novels, poetry and criticism, as well as editor of the *English Review*. *The Good Soldier* is considered his finest work. It is notable for its use of flash-backs and of an unreliable narrator. Furthermore, his novel tetralogy *Parade's End* continues to be admired for its portrayal of World War I.

THE GOOD SOLDIER

A TALE OF PASSION

- **Genre:** novel
- **Reference edition:** Ford, F. M. (2011) *The Good Soldier*. Ware: Wordsworth Classics.
- **1st edition:** 1915
- **Themes:** marriage, society, infidelity, passion, deceit

The first person narrator, John Dowell, tells the story of the relationship between him and his wife, Florence, and another couple, Edward and Leonora Ashburnham, and their ward, Nancy Rufford. John constructs the story through a series of memories, which are not related in chronological order. This technique creates a disjointed narrative; an effect which is deepened by the narrator's shifting perceptions of the characters. In this respect, Ford's novel is a precursor to the experimental novels of high modernism, which are characterised by departures from the traditional narrative coherence of Victorian realism and of conventional Edwardian novels. *The Good*

Soldier continues to excite critical attention. The uncertain ethical atmosphere which pervades the book reflects the loss of social and moral stability felt in the early part of the 20th century, and the account of the turbulent relationships between the characters may be construed as an echo of Ford's own disorderly personal life.

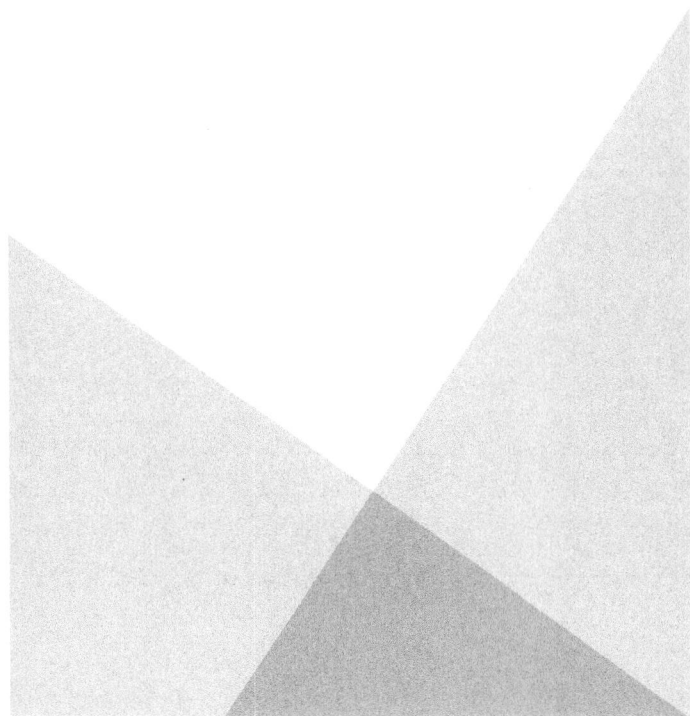

SUMMARY

TWO COUPLES

The novel opens with the narrator, John Dowell, describing the close and comfortable friendship that he and his wife, Florence, enjoyed with Captain Edward Ashburnham and his wife Leonora at the spa of Nauheim in 1904. The Ashburnhams are a well-bred English couple with an estate in Fordingbridge. The Dowells are a wealthy American couple who intended to travel extensively in Europe. However, a storm on the Atlantic crossing causes Florence to have heart problems. For this reason, the couple spend a protracted period at the spa, where Florence receives treatment for her condition.

John explains that much later, in 1913, Edward asks him to come to the estate. There he learns the troubled history of the English couple. The cause of their difficulties is what John describes as Edward's sentimentalism. In bald terms, Edward has a weakness for women. He is initially disgraced by the affair of kissing a servant girl in a railway carriage. This is followed by an affair with a courtesan, the mistress of a Russian noble, who demands a large payment for her services. After making this payment, the Ashburnhams can no longer afford to maintain their estate. They rent the estate and move to Burma, where they are able to live more affordably. Through Leonora's resourcefulness and frugality, and through investing tips given to the likeable Edward, they manage to rebuild their finances. In Burma, Edward forms an attachment to a young and subservient woman, Maisie Maidan, who is married to young officer of little means. Leonora is relieved by this attachment because it is apparent that the passive Maisie will not be troublesome. The young woman has heart problems, and so Leonora offers to pay for her treatment at the spa. Edward fakes a heart problem and he and Leonora accompany Maisie to Nauheim.

The English and American couples are initially brought together through an encounter between Florence and Leonora. Upon opening Edward's letters, Leonora discovers that he is being bribed by the husband of yet another woman he has had an affair with. She later encounters Maisie emerging from Edward's room, and imagining that the lovers have been cavorting happily together, whilst she has been suffering distress over the letter, she slaps Maisie on the cheek. Her bracelet becomes entangled in Maisie's hair and she is struggling to remove it when Florence chances upon the two. Florence disentangles the bracelet, and although Leonora explains the situation away by saying that she had been adjusting Maisie's hair, it is evident from the red mark on the young woman's face, and her tears, that Leonora has just struck her. Thus Leonora is forced to begin her acquaintance with Florence on an intimate footing.

FLORENCE'S SUICIDE

John describes himself as functioning as nurse to his wife. He is constantly concerned with keeping her from emotionally distressing subjects, such as love, crime, and poverty. He is therefore pleased when Florence occupies herself with intellectual and cultural pursuits. Florence takes an interest in educating Edward, and Edward clearly enjoys being educated by Florence. The two begin an affair, of which John is blissfully unaware.

Leonora has a ward, Nancy Rufford, who visits the couple in Nauheim. One evening Nancy and Edward head off to the casino. Leonora remarks that at 22, Nancy now needs a chaperone. She asks Florence to follow and join them.

Edward and Nancy head into the park rather than to the casino. They sit on a bench and are chatting, when Edward is suddenly overcome with the realisation that he is in love with Nancy, and that she is the one great love of his life. He begins to express his admiration for her, but he quickly sees that she takes the compliment as coming from an adored father-figure, rather than a lover, and he curbs his feelings.

John, meanwhile, retires to the lounge and is approached by what he considers a somewhat unsavoury man, who attempts to draw him into conversation. Through the window John observes Florence return, running with her hand on her heart. As she enters the lounge, she sees him conversing with the man and covers her face. She then rushes off to her room. The man then reveals that some years ago he had witnessed Florence emerging from the bedroom of a dissolute man named Jimmy in the early hours of the morning. It is at this point that John realises that Florence has been unfaithful. A few hours later he goes up to her room, where he finds her dead, lying on her bed with a vial in her hand. He assumes that the vial contains her heart medicine and that her heart had been so taxed by the distressing events that the medicine was unable to save her. Immediately after Florence's death, John observes to Leonora that his wife's death puts him in a position to marry Nancy.

EDWARD'S SUICIDE

Leonora tells Nancy that Edward is dying for love of her. Nancy responds that she is dying for love of him. Leonora insists that Nancy should save Edward's life by sacrificing her virtue. Nancy obeys, presenting herself at his bed at night, but he sends her back to her own room.

Edward resolves to send Nancy to her father in India. He accepts that he cannot have Nancy, but he wishes only that she will continue to love him. Leonora is adamant that he should not have even this satisfaction. She informs Nancy of Edward's philandering and of her own suffering at his hands.

Both Edward and Leonora telegram John to visit them, believing that his presence might help soothe the turbulent relations between them all. On the surface they maintain an appearance of reserved composure, even when Nancy departs for India.

After Nancy's departure, Edward begins to recover his equanimity. He stops drinking and becomes constructively involved in the lives of his tenants. One day, at the stables whilst in conversation with John about estate affairs, Edward receives a blithe telegram from Nancy, reporting that she is enjoying her voyage. He takes out his penknife, then he passes the telegram to John and asks him to take it inside to Leonora. John is aware of Edward's intentions, but he goes anyway. Edward commits suicide by slitting his throat.

Nancy loses her reason when, at a stop on the journey, she reads in a newspaper of Edward's suicide. When she arrives in India her father telegrams Leonora asking if she will visit, in the hope that a familiar face will restore her sanity. Leonora asks John to go with Nancy's old nurse, but they are unable to be of any help.

Leonora marries a respectable but boring man, and is expecting a child at the end of the novel. She sells the estate of Branshaw Manor to John, who lives there with Nancy and her nurse, shunning the rest of the world.

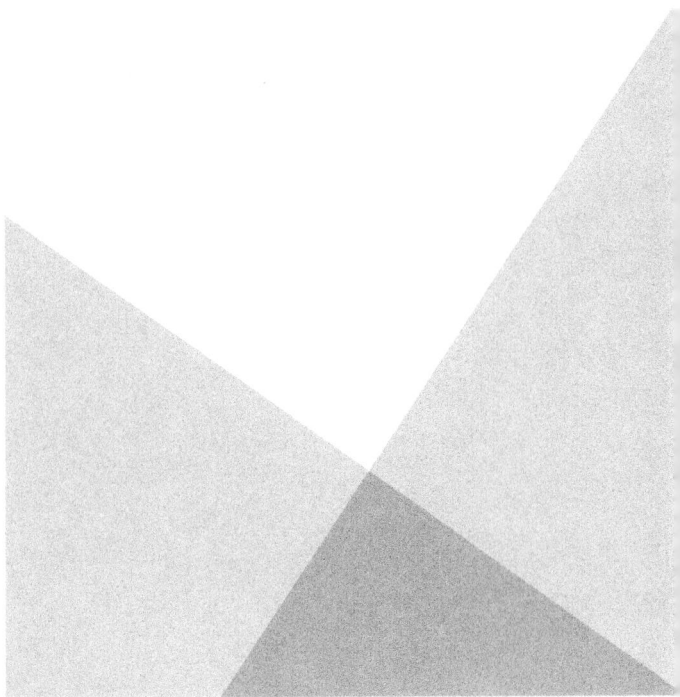

CHARACTER STUDY

JOHN DOWELL

The narrator, John Dowell, mentions more than once that he is a man of wealth and leisure. He sees himself as Florence's nurse, and is constantly preoccupied with preserving the state of her weak heart by keeping her from all disturbing experiences and topics. He reveals his character by describing the reactions of other characters towards him. For example, Maisie is subservient to all, even to him. We also see elements of John's character through his own descriptions of his actions; for example, he reveals his iron-willed resolve in his determined pursuit of Florence as a wife.

Although intelligently observant, he fails to understand Leonora's hint about his wife's affair with Edward. John admits towards the end that he loves Edward, because Edward is himself. In other words, Edward is the man he would have liked to be. He respects Edward for his passion, and views Edward as the victim of a world which tolerates only the normal people, like Leonora, who live conventionally upright lives mediated by small deceits.

FLORENCE

The first thing we learn about 'poor Florence', as John frequently refers to her in the early part of the novel, is that she has a weak heart and that this condition has been caused by a storm at sea during the couple's crossing of the Atlantic to Europe. She is an educated and cultured woman, having studied at Vassar. According to her husband, she dresses well, and expensively, and she has her own money. Florence has been raised by her aunts. When these elderly ladies become aware of the narrator's intentions to marry Florence, they attempt to dissuade him. It appears that there is something about Florence of which he is ignorant, and which they wish to protect him from.

Florence is determined to visit Europe, and it is clear that she accepts the narrator over her other suitors because he is able to make this dream come true for her. They elope and depart for Europe immediately. Florence is ill from the start, and the doctors imply that she should not be subjected to sexual advances from her new husband. Florence continues to suffer from her heart condition, and locks her bedroom door every night; thus, the marriage is never consummated, and John effectively becomes Florence's nurse rather than her husband. As the novel progresses it becomes apparent that Florence has faked her heart condition in order to keep John at bay, so that she can carry out her affairs.

EDWARD

Edward is consistently described by the narrator in terms of the ideal English gentleman. He has a country estate and serves as a magistrate in his parish. John refers to Edward's many understated compassionate acts. He mentions that these acts are often towards those who hold no station in society, and are therefore a testament to his disinterestedness. He particularly notes that Edward has displayed great kindness towards Nancy. He furthermore notes that he reckons that after about three years Edward becomes bored of Florence, but out of a sense of duty and decency, continues to maintain his liaison with her.

Edward is determined not to act on his passion for Nancy. The effort of self-denial drives him to distraction and to drinking.

LEONORA

Unlike John, Leonora is aware of the affair between Edward and Florence right from the start. She had hoped that after Maisie's death, Edward would return to her as a devoted husband. She is encouraged in this when Edward expresses his gratitude for her astute management of their financial affairs. She is, therefore, tortured by his affair with Florence, whom she regards with contempt. As a Catholic, she is unwilling to divorce Edward, and she also dreads the scandal and social stigma of divorce. Unlike Florence, Leonora is restrained and taciturn about private affairs. It is Edward's affair with Florence, however, which drives her to become active and communicative, with devastating consequences.

Leonora realises that Nancy is Edward's great love. She is appalled that Edward could have such feelings for her ward. She makes great efforts to prevent the two from being alone together. As

John sees it, she wishes to protect Nancy. She does, however, realise that, in this case, Edward will restrain himself and that Nancy is at no risk. She is, nevertheless, tormented by Edward's love for Nancy.

NANCY RUFFORD

Edward and Leonora are devoted to Nancy, who came into their care at the age of 13. Nancy is told that her mother has been driven to suicide by her father's ill-temper. She later discovers that, in fact, her mother ran away with another man. She is schooled at a Catholic convent and spends her holidays with the Ashburnhams at their home.

Nancy adores Edward and Leonora and regards their marriage as perfect. As a convent-educated girl, she knows nothing about sex or divorce. By a comment from Leonora she comes to understand that Leonora and Edward are unhappy in their marriage. Through a newspaper article and discussions with Leonora she learns about affairs and divorce. It finally dawns on her that Edward is attracted to her, although she does not understand what this means in physical terms.

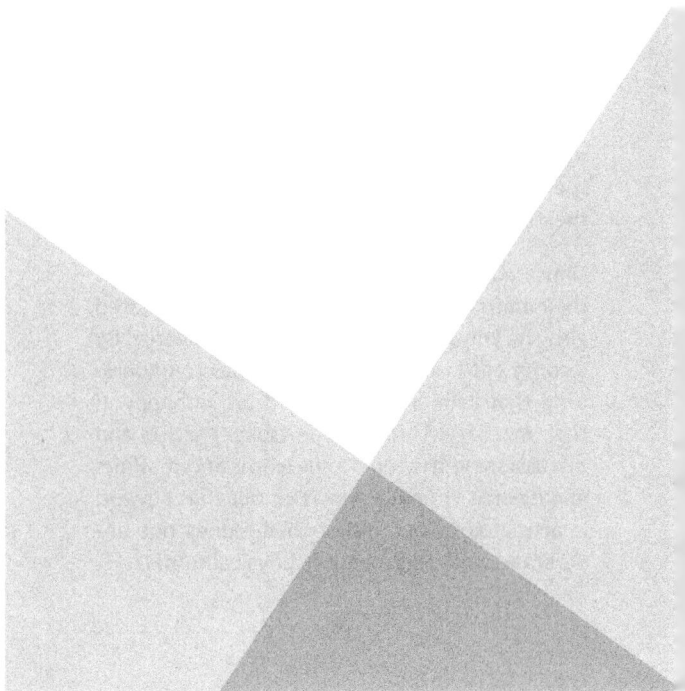

ANALYSIS

MEMORY

The narrator moves back and forth in time between the period beginning in 1904 and spent in Nauheim; the period several months earlier of his courtship of Florence; the year 1913, when he visited Edward and Leonora at their estate in England; and the present of the narration. The novel therefore has a non-linear chronology and is told as a succession of recollections as the narrator attempts to unravel and interpret the progress of the various relationships and the events that determine their progress. He gradually pieces together a narrative based on his own observations, deductions and speculations, and the confidences imparted to him by Edward and Leonora.

For example, it is only years later, when Leonora remarks that she thought Florence foolish to commit suicide, that John learns of Florence's affair with Edward. He also learns that Florence had confided in Leonora that she had a vial containing poison. John had always thought the vial contained heart medication, and had assumed when he found her dead, with the vial in her hand, that she had been attempting to prevent her death, not bringing it about. John then begins to piece together a story on the basis of what both Leonora and Edward tell him and of his own memories of what occurred that evening. It is his supposition that, as Leonora had requested, Florence followed Edward and Nancy out of the hotel with the intention of joining them, so that she could act as chaperone to Nancy. However, following the two into the park, wearing black herself, and unseen by them, the jealous and insecure Florence overhears Edward's declaration of love to Nancy, and this is what causes her to rush back to the hotel. Nevertheless, John believes that it is the shame of his discovery of the affair with Jimmy that in fact drives her to suicide.

NARRATION

When an author tells a story, he or she has to select a point of view from which the account of events and descriptions of characters is given. This is referred to as the narrative mode of the fictional work, and is one of the key factors to consider in the analysis of a novel. The most commonly used modes of narration are third person and first person narratives. In *The Good Soldier* Ford Maddox Ford chooses to use the first person narrative form rather than the third person. In contrast to third person narration, where the narrator is outside the story, a first person narrator, in this case John Dowell, participates in the events. Unlike the third person narrator, who according to tradition is omniscient, the first person narrator is limited. Typically, and according to convention, the omniscient narrator's account and judgements are accepted as authoritative. However, as a first person narrator, John is invariably unreliable, for he relates things only as he interprets them. Other interpretations may, of course, be made, and John does occasionally point out the possibility that he may be wrong.

As he considers the relationship between the two couples in retrospect, John observes that although they spent a great amount of time together and enjoyed each other's company, they never grew sufficiently intimate for him to know the private details of the Ashburnhams' lives.

He puts this down to the Ashburnhams being English. The reader may argue, however, that John's ignorance of the affairs about him, in spite of Leonora's hints, suggests either a deliberate obtuseness, or an extreme naivety on his part.

Although the narrator is a participant in the action, he is primarily concerned with recounting the experiences of others. John, along with the characters he portrays, provokes varying, and sometimes contradictory, responses. One may feel sympathy for John, at other times frustration with him, and yet again at other times one may feel chilled by his detachment in the face of the emotional devastation around him. These responses will also depend on the reader and on a range of factors such as the reader's gender or their attitudes towards Catholicism, to name only two.

MODERNISM

Modernism is generally considered to have been a cultural movement prominent in the early part of the 20th century. In particular, the movement reflects responses to the anarchy and futility of World War I and is characterised by a sense that traditional forms were no longer adequate to represent reality. Earlier assumptions of the stability of Western society needed to be rejected in order to accurately depict the society of the time. Modernist authors therefore experimented with subject matter and with the formal properties of literature.

Whilst *The Good Soldier* cannot be considered a fully modernist text, it may be seen as a precursor to the modernist experiment and as containing elements suggestive of modernism. It departs from the conventional assumptions of Edwardian literature in that it portrays character as elusive and lacking coherence. Although John attempts to analyse and explain the motives and behaviours of the various characters, the exact truth remains obscure, and the reader is left, ultimately, to draw his or her own conclusions. For example, John claims that Leonora subjects Edward to emotional torture by revealing his infidelities to Nancy, so that the younger woman will cease to respect and love him. At the conclusion of the novel he states emphatically that he dislikes Leonora. Nevertheless, earlier in the novel he is sympathetic to Leonora's position as a betrayed wife, and represents her suffering so vividly as to justify her ultimate loss of composure and her vindictive behaviour.

In the novel, people and events are not necessarily what they appear, and this applies to the narrator as well. John represents himself as an innocent and as the victim of a deceitful and unfaithful wife. However, there are accounts which reveal dubious elements of his own personality and which may suggest alternative interpretations. For example, he recounts an incident when he shocks Florence by beating an elderly and devoted black servant of his who had failed to look after her medications properly. He observes, rather lightly, that upon seeing the potential violence of his reactions, Florence may have been afraid of him.

FURTHER REFLECTION

SOME QUESTIONS TO THINK ABOUT...

- Which narrative method does Ford employ? What effects does the author achieve with this method of narration, and what are its strengths and limitations?
- How does the author signal that John Dowell is potentially unreliable as a witness and as a narrator?
- Do you agree with John's interpretation of the destruction of the Ashburnhams' marriage and of Edward's eventual suicide? Which factors influence your personal response to John's narration?
- How does the author use memory in the construction of the narrative and what are the effects of telling the story in this manner?
- How does Ford characterise John?
- Compare the narrator's treatment of Edward's affairs and suicide with his treatment of Florence.

- In what ways does John's attitude towards the characters shift? With which character, if any, does John retain a constant sympathy?
- How does the reader's response to John shift as the narrative progresses?

We want to hear from you!
Leave a comment on your online library
and share your favourite books on social media!

FURTHER READING

REFERENCE EDITION

- Ford, F. M. (2011) *The Good Soldier*. Ware: Wordsworth Classics.

REFERENCE STUDIES

- Abrams, M. H. (1999) *A Glossary of Literary Terms*. Fort Worth: Harcourt Brace.

www.brightsummaries.com

Ebook EAN: 9782808019262

Paperback EAN: 9782808019279

Legal Deposit: D/2019/12603/130

Cover: © Primento

Digital conception by Primento, the digital partner of
publishers.

Printed in Great Britain
by Amazon